"It is all the same, drawing, painting, modelling, the irresistible desire to copy any beautiful object which strikes the eye. Why cannot one be content to look at it? I cannot rest, I must draw, however poor the result..."

Painting of Beatrix Potter in 1938 by D. Banner

Beatrix Potter

BEATRIX POTTER

Creator of Peter Rabbit

•

By Peter Durwood

FOREWORD BY SUSAN STICKNEY-BAILEY, PH.D.

1333 — June 1991

THE KIPLING PRESS • NEW YORK

Printed in the United States
ISBN 0-943718-09-0

The Kipling Press
First Edition

FOREWORD

Why should someone who has seemingly out-grown tiny picture-books read about the life of Beatrix Potter? Almost all of us have read her story about a rabbit named Peter who went into Mr. McGregor's garden. Some of us may even know all twenty-three of her little tales, whose heroes and heroines are hedgehogs, mice, frogs, kittens or pigs. Although they were written for small children, these stories stay in our memories long after we have read them. Beatrix Potter's books—with their beautifully painted watercolors—are memorable because they are good stories.

A good story is one in which the main character overcomes great difficulties. The characters in Beatrix Potter's stories always escape from some tight spot. Beatrix Potter's life is a lot like her stories—she had her own difficulties to overcome. The special quality of her stories may come from the way Beatrix Potter handled the difficult circumstances of her own life. For instance, her stories have helped some of us to form our ideas of what makes a cozy and comfortable home. Yet Beatrix Potter did not have a home that was cozy or comfortable until she was almost fifty years old—when she made one for herself!

Beatrix Potter was born in 1866. At that time women were not allowed to go to school. They were kept at home and were sometimes taught by a governess. Beatrix had a good mind, but her talents were not encouraged. Her parents did not pay much attention to Beatrix and her older brother, except to make sure the children were obedient and proper, according to the strict standards of that time. After her brother was sent off to school he spent as little time in his parents' home as possible, so Beatrix was left very much alone. No one thought to help her to make friends or to mix with other people. She became shy and spent long hours by herself on the top floor of her parents' cold and formal house.

Beatrix Potter was interested in everything around her, especially art and natural history. She combined the two interests by learning to draw exactly the plants and animals she collected or saw in natural history museums. She developed an interest in mushrooms and made hundreds of drawings of many species during summer trips in the country with her parents. She also smuggled home little animals she caught in the country. She kept them, along with other animals she found in her London neighborhood, in her lonely upstairs room. She spent hours observing her little animals and drawing them. These creatures—hedgehogs, newts, toads, mice, and two rabbits named Peter and Benjamin—not only provided her with material for her studies, they also became her friends. Her toad lived on her desk for a whole year. Beatrix came to know her animals in two ways: by studying their natural habits, and by learning their individual personalities.

When she was in her teens, she began to desire to see something come of her work and her abilities. An uncle tried to help her get the recognition she deserved for several discoveries she had made in the field of natural history. However, scientists would not recognize the work of a woman who had never been to school and had no university degree.

When she was almost thirty, she began writing "picture letters" to the small children of one of her former governesses. In these letters she would make up adventures to describe the doings of her animal pets, then illustrate them. Most of the stories take place in the Lake District near London where Beatrix grew up. The pictures were wonderful examples of Beatrix's power of observation and skill as a painter, as well as of her sense of humor and imagination. It was from these letters that her books grew. Children became just the right audience for her knowledge of animals and her ability to create fantasy. When she couldn't find a publisher for her first book, *The Tale of Peter Rabbit*, she published it at her own expense. Before long, her books became very popular and have been enjoyed ever since.

Beatrix Potter succeeded in developing her talents despite the limitations placed upon her by her parents and by the times in which she lived. Today her books appeal to children all over the world, who live in times and places vastly different from those Beatrix Potter knew when she wrote her stories. Her books are about day-to-day life, and her fanciful animal characters remain true to their animal natures. Perhaps her stories are still popular because they are real, and because they contain truths about what is important in life.

— *Susan Stickney, Ph.D.*
Santa Fe, New Mexico
March 2, 1988

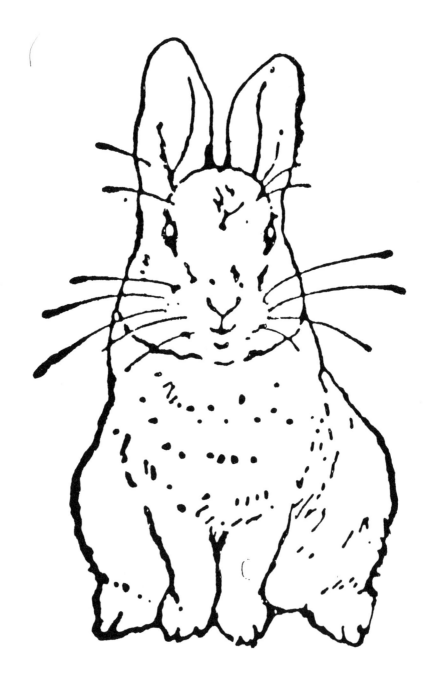

From The Tale of Peter Rabbit, *1901*

A SPECIAL WRITER, A SPECIAL ARTIST

"Once upon a time there were four little Rabbits, and their
names were — Flopsy, Mopsy, Cotton-tail, and Peter."

What makes a children's book good? Like everyone, children love a good story that is both interesting enough to hold their attention and simple enough for them to understand. Most of all, children are naturally curious; they like to learn about new things.

Beatrix Potter had a great knack for combining these elements with beautiful drawings of her characters that made her stories come alive for young readers. Her books are enjoyed as much by today's children as they were by the children for whom she wrote nearly a century ago—a fact

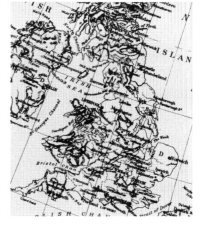

that proves her great talent for touching the hearts and minds of very young people.

In her own time, Beatrix Potter's classic picture books raised the standards of both writing and illustration in children's literature. This book is about her life and how she created her famous tales. But in order to help us appreciate the effect she had, let's take a brief glimpse at the history of children's literature.

Before children's books came on the scene, young people had to look to adult books for their entertainment. The first books printed in Britain were popular stories from oral tradition—stories that had circulated by word of mouth to the point where everyone knew them: *Reynard the Fox* appeared in 1481, followed by *The Fables of Aesop* in 1484. These were soon joined by books like *Robin Hood* and *King Arthur*, books that were enjoyed by adults but that captured the imagination of children with their spirit of adventure. Children also took to the adventure in another book written for grown-ups—*Pilgrim's Progress*, by John Bunyan, which appeared in 1678. (After this unexpected success, Bunyan actually *tried* to write a book he thought the young would enjoy, a collection of instructional rhymes. Children, however, did not like it; the book had no story.)

Meanwhile, children were grabbing up more stories written for adult readers; both *Robinson Crusoe* (1719) and *Gulliver's Travels* (1726) appealed to children because they're about what it's like to find yourself in a strange new world—which is the way the real world often seems to a very young child.

Children's literature first appeared in Britain around the late 1600s or early 1700s. Soon a great debate emerged about the value of "fun" children's books versus that of "educational" ones. In the 1700s, the outcome of the debate was influenced by the dawn of "The Age of Reason," a time marked by the exciting scientific theories of men like Sir Isaac Newton. As these scientific discoveries challenged the colorful myths of the British people, children's books lost their air of excitement and adventure and instead became stiff parables that taught morals and codes of proper behavior.

Late in the century, the far-sighted poet William Blake argued against such books, saying that children should be respected as individuals who had their own way of looking at things rather than regarded as stupid miniature people who had to be taught to act like adults.

It wasn't until the mid-1800s, though, that publishers began to heed Blake's words. In the 1840s, the first English translation of the Hans Christian Anderson stories was printed, as was the fine series of illustrated classics, the "Home Treasury." In the 1860s the *Alice in Wonderland* books appeared, and a decade later printer Edmund Evans and a small group of talented artists produced the first great picture books, which paved the way for Beatrix Potter.

Beatrix Potter was both a gifted artist and a great writer. Her words and pictures always tell a simple story that is filled with meaningful detail. Her animals make fine subject matter for children's books because they reflect many of a child's natural traits: curiosity, intuition, a love of beauty, and the ability to give tremendous amounts of affection.

She could build an entire story on the natural personality of an animal—for example, the orderly hedgehog Mrs. Tiggy-Winkle, or the scatterbrained Jemima Puddle-Duck. No less realistic are her illustrations. The characters—the animals themselves—are drawn with an accuracy and feeling that could come only by having spent many hours watching animals go about their business.

The humor and liveliness in the words Beatrix Potter used to narrate the stories and those that her characters speak tell us something about the times in which she lived. Many of the words are long and have many syllables; these are used to gently poke fun at some of the stuck-up behavior of people in her own Victorian England.

Beatrix Potter never "talked down" to her young readers but instead took them seriously as equals. It is no coincidence that everything about Beatrix Potter's books seems perfectly suited to the taste of children. It was a taste she truly shared; this is what makes her work so special.

CHILDHOOD

"Then as we struggle on, the thoughts of that
peaceful past time of childhood comes to us like
soft music and a blissful vision through the snow."

E ven by Victorian standards, Beatrix Potter's childhood was extreme, and in many ways it lasted until she was nearly forty. She was born on July 28, 1866, and for the first five years of her life, she was an only child. She grew up in Bolton Gardens, at that time a well-to-do district in the South Kensington area of London. Her parents were both independently wealthy from the earnings of their merchant-class parents—the Potters did not exactly know what to do with themselves, and, perhaps to make up for the emptiness of their lives, they lived under the most rigid control possible.

Every second of every day ran like clockwork, and every day was the same: they would all eat breakfast together, hardly speaking at all—then both parents would leave the house for much of the day, Mr. Potter going to his club to read the paper and chat, and Mrs. Potter going for drives in the afternoon. Beatrix was left with a nurse who brought her the same lunch and took her on the same walk every day—not a particularly full life.

LL CUNDIFF

The only family outings occurred at Easter, when they would spend three weeks at the shore, and at summertime, when they would transplant the life at Bolton Gardens to Scotland, and resume the clockwork. The main reason they went to Scotland was to provide Mr. Potter with a change of scenery and, at least for three months a year, a house that would attract more visitors than Bolton Gardens did.

Clearly vitality had skipped a generation in the Potter family. Mr. Potter was proud of his father's money and connections, not of the fact that he had been a hard worker who, through sheer labor, built himself a second fortune after the first one had crumbled. He had been a man of great integrity who embodied the ideals of the Victorian period, having a firm belief in the value of education and the pursuit of science. Likewise, Jessie Crompton, Beatrix's maternal grandmother, was a lively character who provided one of the precious few inspirations of Beatrix's childhood; Beatrix was fascinated by her stories about the Crompton family, and would listen from a secret spot under the table when she was young. When she was old enough for an "official" seat at the table, she quietly recorded every detail of the stories she heard on scraps of paper, including the exact words Jessie used. Beatrix respected the strength and outspokenness of her grandmother's personality; she liked to think that she had inherited that integrity.

The birth of Beatrix's brother, Bertram, did not ultimately affect her isolation, for, as soon as he was old enough, he was off at school. Beatrix was later taught at home, since girls were not generally sent to school. Beatrix was not upset at not going to school; she did not welcome the thought of suffering the pressure at school, or the possibility of losing her individuality. She was very protective of herself and her privacy—in the presence of company she felt ill at ease, and would withdraw. But she did feel at ease in the company of Miss Hammond, her governess, who gave her much support in her pursuits of nature and her efforts in drawing. Miss Hammond soon felt that she had served her purpose, though, and left after only a few years. Clearly the most educational, and invigorating, part of Beatrix's early childhood was the annual escape to Scotland.

The first summer in Scotland was a revelation for the children. Here, in the northlands, the ancestral home of the Cromptons was a place where beauty reigned and Real Life took place—it was their first, and emotionally, their final step out of their life at Bolton Gardens, where there was simply nothing for them to enjoy. Immediately Beatrix and Bertram began drinking in every facet of their surroundings: the animals, the cottages, the farms, the workers in the fields—and they felt as if they belonged in that world. Beatrix had always had a vivid memory, as she much later noted: "I can remember quite plainly from one and two years old; not only facts, like learning to walk, but places and sentiments—the way things impressed a very young child." Her great memory must have especially clung to her impressions on this first important visit to the Northlands.

She and Bertram became enthusiastic collectors of things from nature: plants, insects, and animals, alive and dead. Once, they actually skinned a dead animal and boiled the skeleton clean in order to study it. These children were not cruel—if anything, this shows how strongly they held an interest in these animals; they had never before been given anything that truly fascinated them. They made paintings and drawings of what they had found, stitching the pictures together into little booklets. Even as a very young child, before she had actually seen any animals, Beatrix was interested in them, and she copied drawings of them from primers.

At one point Beatrix and Bertram tried their hand at printing with an old printing press they found. In the absence of ink they had to improvise to make their own, using a mixture of soot and colza oil to apply to their own woodcuts. Upon receiving some messily—although earnestly—printed gifts, the adults took away the ink, fearing a catastrophic mess.

One of the people who visited in Scotland was John Bright, a Quaker orator who had been a friend of Mr. Potter's father. He had a wonderful voice, and he read poetry to Beatrix and Bertram, another element of unusual beauty in the country, which they greatly enjoyed.

Beatrix in 1881 with her friend Spot

ART AND SCIENCE

*"Nature has probably never appeared alike to two artists.
They are all more or less right in their own views."*

Upon the Potters' return to Bolton Gardens, Beatrix fell back into solitude. Bertram was back at school, she did not accompany her mother on the daily drives, and no companions were invited for tea. She found her only solace in her pets, of which she had many, and her drawing. Such was her need for company that she had a veritable menagerie that included mice, snails, bats, a rabbit, and a hedgehog.

Beatrix became more and more introverted as her solitude continued through her adolescence. She drew many sketches, and pressed flowers from Scotland. Sometimes she walked to the nearby Natural History Museum, to draw the animals and

LL CUNDIFF

skeletons there. Animals came to be brought along on family vacations, sometimes secretly; she would carry a rabbit under her arm, and use the rabbit's cage as a suitcase.

Beatrix ultimately endured adolescence with no real guidance or attention from her parents. She had received little more as a child, but now she was approaching adulthood. She was on her way to becoming a grown woman, and as a woman at that time, the Victorian era, her future options were very limited: she could either get married or become a spinster. A career was out of the question.

After Bertram had finished school he decided to become an artist, which was in keeping with the family's generally keen interest in pictures. Naturally, his favorite subject matter was the Scottish countryside, and it was a matter of course for him to move back in with his parents and to paint during the summers—though his mind would soon change about how close he wanted to live to his parents.

Mr. Potter frequently visited art exhibits, and, after a while, took Beatrix as well. As they regarded the paintings Beatrix would write down her own reactions to them, studying every technical detail; her tastes were very clear, and very strong. Overall she looked for a feeling of realness: the animals and people must be accurately rendered, and there must be a good sense of perspective. The color must have richness and depth; it must not be flatly applied. And not everything should be equally in focus; the objects 'closest' to us should be crystal-clear, and 'farther' objects should become progressively hazier.

She seemed to be looking for a style of painting that created a convincing reality. If the details of a picture were unrealistic or too obviously subjective, then the spell would be broken, as when seeing the ventriloquist's lips move, or when seeing the puppeteer's hands. The picture must be subtle and seamless; it can only work on you if you do not realize that it is working. This perfectly describes the art Beatrix Potter came to produce for her books: even though a mouse in a coat and glasses seems like a subjective or unrealistic image, it works, because the mouse is so thoroughly a mouse, and the coat and glasses so thoroughly coat and glasses (even though mouse-sized), that it all looks exactly as it should—as it would if it *were* real.

Beatrix's interests in natural detail were leading her into geology and other scientific fields of study. She would use a microscope to study features of mold. She also became interested in fossils, at first drawing the ones she saw in museums, then photographing and collecting her own.

Her ultimate scientific interest was in fungus, about which she was genuinely excited. She had spent years making a large number of very fine drawings of different types of fungi, which she classified herself, and hoped to publish as a book. Her parents gave her no support whatsoever in the undertaking of this important project. But she did have a helpful uncle, Sir Henry Roscoe, who held some clout in the field of science, and he arranged for Beatrix to meet, among others, the director of the Royal Botanic Gardens. Lest her parents keep her from going, Beatrix snuck out of the house to attend the meeting.

She was greeted with defensiveness and a fair amount of condescension by the director and his colleagues. Far from applauding or welcoming her interests in the field, they dismissed her drawings as having no scientific value whatsoever, only because she did not use diagrams. They also took offense at the fact that a *woman*, of all people, was experimenting and theorizing on her own, outside the scientific community. Beatrix had a theory that lichens were not a separate and new life form, but a combination of two preexisting forms of life—fungus and algae. Her idea was immediately rejected by the scientists; later, by someone else, her theory was found to be absolutely correct. Beatrix, of course, was in a difficult situation as a woman during that period of history, and she must have experienced a great deal of frustration simply in trying to express herself.

After this discouraging treatment, Beatrix's uncle encouraged her to try again and to write a paper on mold spores, which he kindly insisted on proofreading for her. Someone else had to read it to the Linnaean Society of London for her, as her gender remained an obstacle. Ultimately, however, nothing more came of this project, either. Beatrix finally felt that any further effort in this field was doomed, so with nothing better to do, she turned her energy back to drawing animals, inspired by the illustrations of Randolph Caldecott.

She considered this only a pastime, but she received encouraging responses from the children she first made pictures for, as well as support from her brother, Bertram, and a family friend, Canon H. D. Rawnsley. Canon Rawnsley was a very accomplished man, energetic and not self-conscious, with interests that overlapped Beatrix's: he was an educated and caring individual, a published author and poet many times over, and a passionate conservationist and lover of nature—Beatrix may as well have been looking at her future self.

From Ginger & Pickles, *1909*

THE SECRET JOURNAL

"A diary, however private, brings back distinctly the
memory of what . . . seemed like a most pleasant dream."

We know about Beatrix Potter's life from her
teens to her thirties only by the discovery of
her private journal. The journal is a collection of notes and observations she had made
to herself, all recorded in a secret code, written in tiny writing on varied pieces of
paper ranging from exercise books to
scraps. She had developed the code as a
young girl, and delighted in the fact
that she could write down thoughts
that no one else could ever know.

The journal was not discovered until
1952, in a drawer in the attic of Castle
Cottage, Beatrix's adult home. It was
found by Mrs. Stephanie Duke, who

had inherited the property after the death of her cousin Beatrix. In the same year, Leslie Linder, a collector of Beatrix Potter's works, learned of the journal's existence, and sought to decipher it. After several years without success, the code was cracked. It took several more years to transcribe the journal. *The Journal of Beatrix Potter* was published in 1966, one hundred years after Beatrix Potter's birth.

The question immediately arose as to why she kept her journal so secret when one finds nothing especially earth shattering or out of the ordinary recorded in it. Beatrix most likely just enjoyed privacy for its own sake. And much of what she wrote indicates subtly that the years of transition from adolescence to adulthood were difficult for her.

She mourned for her lost childhood, for, even though much of it was emotionally unsatisfying and spent in solitude, she cherished the few adults in her world who had doted on her. When she was no longer a child, she felt she could no longer command even that small amount of attention. It is not surprising that her will to exert herself in life was sometimes tentative, when her present life was so unsatisfying and seemed to have no promise of changing. At 19 she wrote, "Oh, life—wearisome, disappointing, and yet in many shades so sweet, I wonder why one is so unwilling to let go this old year?—not because it has been joyful, but because I fear its successors—I am terribly afraid of the future."

But Beatrix loved her privacy dearly for the freedom it gave her to express herself without being judged—and the secret code was a guarantee that she could say whatever she wanted. No matter how trivial; and no one would ever be able to interfere. She felt that drawing lessons, for example, which her parents did provide for her, were an interference, and she confided to her journal: "It is tiresome, when you do get some lessons, to be taught in a way you dislike and to have to swallow your feelings out of considerations at home." For Beatrix, drawing in solitude provided her with a reason to live and a way to ward off depression. It seemed a part of her nature; she wrote: "It is all the same, drawing, painting, modelling, the irresistible desire to copy any beautiful object which strikes the eye. Why cannot one be content to look at it? I cannot rest, I *must* draw, however poor the result . . . " And so about painting she wrote, "I don't want lessons, I want practice. I hope it is not pride that makes me so stiff against teaching, but a bad or indifferent teacher is worse than none. It cannot be taught."

When Beatrix was about twenty, she contracted rheumatic fever, a contagious disease that causes heart damage. The disease caused her to lose most of her hair; it left her enervated and in great pain, effects which lingered over the next two years. The fever completely derailed her drawing and writing: "Part of the time I was too ill, and since then the laziness and unsettledness consequent on weakness have so demoralized me, that I have persevered in nothing for more than a week at a time except toothache."

Fortunately Beatrix ultimately recovered and resumed her life; her parents, however, were becoming quite an obstacle to her freedom. Since her illness she would scarcely leave the house without encountering resistance, because of their new concern for her health. And, apparently, the effects of her parents' own uninspiring life-style were beginning to tell. As Beatrix delicately put it, when commenting on vacation time at the Potters': "It is somewhat trying to pass a season of enjoyment in the company of persons who are constantly on the outlook for matters of complaint."

As her parents grew more bored and listless, Beatrix was determined to fill her own confinement with stimulating activity. Besides painting, drawing, and reading, she took on the task of memorizing the Shakespeare plays, line for line, in her late twenties: "I know *Richard III* right through, *Henry VI* four fifths, *Richard II* except three pages, *King John* four acts, a good half the *Midsummer Night's Dream* and *The Tempest*, half way through *The Merchant of Venice* and *Henry VIII*. . .I learnt six more or less in a year. Never felt the least strained or should not have done it."

From The Tale of Little Pig Robinson, *1930*

As happy as Beatrix was in her productive solitude she also welcomed certain friendly visitors, as evidenced by several "visitations" she received while learning *Henry VIII*: "The 4th Act is associated with the company of a robin who came in at daylight attracted by sleepy flies, and sat on the curtain-pole or the wardrobe, bold and black-eyed. He only once sang. The swallows used to fly round the next room. Mice were also an amusement and extremely tame, picking up crumbs from the table."

In 1890 Beatrix sent some rabbit illustrations to a publishing firm, including the names of the characters in the pictures, hoping that they might be used as Christmas cards. The publishers, Hildesheimer and Faulkner, liked the pictures and hired Frederic Weatherly, a popular songwriter, to supply some simple verses for the illustrations. The result, called *A Happy Pair*, was not so much a book as an elaborate Christmas card, believed to have appeared at Christmastime of 1890. It is very rare to find now, and difficult to trace to its year of publication. It has seven pages, with a heavier page as the cover; the pages have golden edges and are not bound, but fastened, by a colored cord.

It is fairly typical of children's literature and packaging at the time. The verses are bland, and the illustrations do not have the strength of Beatrix's later work. Largely because she was emulating Caldecott's work, they possess his cartoon characteristics more than her own. Also, the method of reproduction did not do justice to her watercolors.

That was the first and last time she illustrated any work but her own. After she was famous her publishers, Frederick Warne & Co., brought up the proposition of illustrating a book someone else had written, but she refused, saying that it would distract her from her own drawing. And, much later in life, she denied ever having illustrated anyone else's work.

Reproduction of Beatrix's actual letter to Noel Moore

THE LETTERS

"I do not remember a time when I did not try to invent
pictures and make for myself a fairyland amongst the
wild flowers, the animals, fungi, mosses, woods and
streams, all the thousand objects of the countryside."

T he wellspring of Beatrix's own remarkable
creations was to flow from a source she had
created years earlier. When she was seven-
teen, she had met Annie Carter, a young
woman just slightly older than Beatrix who
had been hired to teach her German. Beatrix took a great liking
to Annie, who had a great deal of independence; she had

traveled extensively, and visited
such places as Germany; and more
importantly, she supported herself.

Shortly after the lessons began,
Annie had a sudden romance and
decided to get married and have
lots of children. Beatrix kept in
touch with Annie, and as each
new child came along, she traveled
out to their home in Wandsworth
to visit them. Beatrix became close

with each child; she had kept so much of her own childhood alive inside her that it was easy for her to relate to the children.

Perhaps Beatrix saw in children companions who mirrored her own enthusiasm and appreciation for animals and other things in nature. In the presence of such kindred spirits, her own desires and abilities to express herself must have been greatly strengthened. The children certainly reflected the attention she showed them; they found her to be exciting, as well as caring company. It was for this special audience that Beatrix Potter began to reveal her world in its greatest clarity.

When Noel, Annie's first child, suffered a prolonged sickness at five, Beatrix began writing letters to him as a comfort, telling him about her activities, and about her pet rabbit, Peter. Elaborating the words here and there would be a drawing or two—in her case, both talents surfaced together. Sometimes she just told a story:

Eastwood, Dunkeld
Sep 4th, 93

My Dear Noel,

I don't know what to write to you, so I shall tell you a story about four little rabbits, whose names were Flopsy, Mopsy, Cottontail, and Peter.

They lived with their Mother in a sand bank under the root of a big fir tree.

'Now, my dears,' said old Mrs. Bunny, 'you may go into the field or down the lane, but don't go into Mr. McGregor's garden . . .'

The story continues to unfold simply and precisely as her mind's eye dictated the key pictures, which are laid out naturally around the lively text. The pictures or words alone have a perfect continuity; together they weave a complete spell.

Letters to Noel's siblings and various other children contained kernels she would later expand as well, stories about characters called Squirrel Nutkin, Mrs. Tiggy-Winkle, and Mr. Jeremy Fisher, among others. The children instantly took the letters to heart, regarding these characters as beloved friends. They loved them enough to have preserved them, so that many exist today.

When Beatrix had written these letters, they caused such a stir among friends that she decided to try publishing one of them as a book. She thought of the letter she had written Noel during his illness eight years earlier—Noel still had it, and he lent it to her to copy. She added some new pictures and text, keeping everything else the same. And throughout this project, she was heartily encouraged by Canon Rawnsley.

After several rejections from publishers Beatrix decided to publish *The Tale of Peter Rabbit* herself. Her tastes dictated what the book would look like. It was small, child-size, which was unusual then, even in children's books. The text appeared on each page, in "bites" of one or two sentences, and every page-turn brought a new picture, a simple line drawing, uncolored, in the style of the letter. The book came out much like the original letter—simply expanded to become a miniature book.

Two hundred and fifty copies appeared in December of 1901, looking splendid in print. Beatrix sold copies to family and friends, who were delighted with the novelty. Since the book had come out so well, she also sent a copy to Frederick Warne & Co. at Canon Rawnsley's recommendation; of all the publishers she had contacted previously, they had actually shown some interest. The book was becoming very popular, so she had 200 more copies printed.

After the Warnes contacted Beatrix and proposed a version of her book with color illustrations, the Potter home suddenly came to life with activity. Beatrix was keenly aware of the new issues that arose, particularly regarding the fact that she knew very little about the publishing business, and that if she did not wish to be controlled by her father (who had strong opinions about publishing), she had better learn. She was also not sure whether she should simply color the illustrations she already had for the Warnes' book, or create new pictures entirely. She actively corresponded by letter with the Warnes, openly expressing her feelings and questions about the matters as they arose. They discussed such topics as the economics involved, the printing processes available, and possible weaknesses in the artwork.

Beatrix stayed at her brother's farm in Scotland for a time to work on the art. Bertram and she both felt that she needed work on drawing people, so she practiced, using the farmhands as models. Bertram's farm at Roxburghshire proved to be an excellent retreat for both of them, a chance for solitude as well as a chance to be together—a pleasant new version of the family vacations, without the parents. Beatrix's doubts about her work fell away as the farm's beauty poured into her, uplifting her, and spilling out into the new illustrations.

That momentum carried her into her next book, *The Tailor of Gloucester*, which was based on a strange incident she had heard of during a stay with one of her cousins, Caroline Hutton. Caroline was, at 25, three years younger than Beatrix, and a great deal more political in her thinking. Like Annie, she gave Beatrix an example of female independence—she was ahead of her time in her disdain for religion and marriage and, just as uncommon, her concern for the poor living conditions of laborers.

Beatrix enjoyed Caroline's company very much, but naturally could not embrace some of her ideas: " . . . I hold an old-fashioned notion that a happy marriage is the crown of a woman's life, and that it is unwise on the part of a nice-looking young lady to proclaim a pronounced dislike of babies and all child cousins." Beatrix's fondness and sensitivity for children, as well as her need for an emotionally satisfying home life, were too central to her character to be compromised.

As to the story, which she heard from some visitors to Caroline's house, it told of a tailor in Gloucester who, before closing his shop one Saturday, had laid out the pieces of a coat that he planned to assemble later. When he returned on Monday, he discovered that the coat had been put together, and the sewing finished—except for a single buttonhole. Pinned to the coat was a note that said, simply, "No more twist."

After she had heard the story, Beatrix accompanied the family on an outing to Gloucester, where she found the street where the tailor supposedly lived and "to everyone's amusement sat down on a doorstep and began to sketch it." Beatrix also sketched some very nice interior scenes from the cottages Caroline showed her in town.

She saw a tailor in Chelsea whom she thought would make a perfect model for her main character. She then pulled off a button from her coat so that she could properly enter the shop and observe him while he sewed the button back on, taking in details for later drawings. Meanwhile, another of Annie's children had fallen ill, and it was she, Freda, who received the original version of *The Tailor of Gloucester*, written in a composition book with the pictures glued in. Beatrix also included a letter that was to become the dedication to the version of the book the rest of us know:

> *My Dear Freda,*
>
> *Because you are fond of fairy tales, and have been ill, I have made you a story all for yourself—a new one that nobody has read before.*
>
> *And the queerest thing about it is—that I heard it in Gloucestershire, and that it is true—at least about the tailor, the waistcoat, and the*
> *'No more twist!'*

Beatrix had a great affection for this story and felt sure it would make a wonderful book. She was not so sure what the Warnes would think of it—they might wish to make changes—so she had five hundred copies printed in color with her own money. Her opinion on the book wavered after it had come out, although she eventually held it most dear. In her correspondence with Norman Warne she wrote, ". . . I was rather afraid people might laugh at the words," and she expressed her fear that the story might "fall rather flat." The Warnes published *The Tailor of Gloucester* in 1903, but without the songs and rhymes of the mice that appeared in her original version—the sacrifice that Beatrix had dreaded, but accepted as "just."

Beatrix completed *The Tale of Squirrel Nutkin*, a story about squirrels that swim and worship an owl, after showing several different versions to children to see which words worked best; she also had to procure some squirrely models for her sketches. When the Warnes's *Nutkin* came out in 1903, Beatrix was deluged with mail from her young fans, who loved, but could not spell "scell nuckin."

From The Roly-Poly Pudding, *1908*

THE BATTLE FOR AUTONOMY

"I have never quite understood the secret of Peter's perennial charm. Perhaps it is because he and his little friends keep on their way, busily absorbed with their own doings."

Beatrix was always pleased and surprised that her books were so popular; getting rich was certainly not her concern. She said herself that she preferred cheap books, explaining, "all my little friends happen to be shilling people," and expressing her dislike of expensive gifts for children. However, this is not to say that Beatrix did not enjoy making her own money, or that she did not value the new purpose she had found. She was beginning to have her own life, and she knew it. She wrote excited letters to Norman Warne, the youngest son of the firm's founder, Frederick; Norman had be-

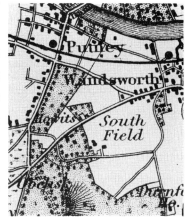

come her main point of contact at the publishers. They discussed future prospects for books, and arranged a conference, but Beatrix was forced abruptly to cancel it much against her will—evidently because of her parents' disapproval. Beatrix's parents, for whatever reason, were tragically destructive in their behavior towards their daughter: whether out of jealousy, outrage, or misguided concern, they fought her growing independence, and proudly opposed her flowering relationship with Norman Warne, whom they considered "beneath her."

Norman Warne was the youngest of five children. He and his sister, Millie, lived with their widowed mother in the family home at Bedford Square, in which they also located their publishing business. Beatrix visited often and found the house to be a warm and comfortable place for her, not exactly something she was used to. She found Mrs. Warne to be of happy spirits, and Millie was of a low-key temperament similar to Beatrix's own—a very good match. The whole family would often gather at the house, and the scores of their children got to know Beatrix.

Beatrix and Norman got along very well. He was quick to perceive the quality of her work, and offered her much thoughtful observation and constructive criticism. She in turn responded to the sensitivity of his comments, and came to seek his opinions more and more, no matter how spontaneous or trivial the issue.

She kept in close contact with Norman as she was working on the pictures for the second version of *The Tailor of Gloucester*. To him she expressed her delight in the discovery of the beautiful antique clothing at what is now The Victoria and Albert Museum—and she used the exhibits as models for the exquisite coat and waistcoat we see in the book. She also told him of the glowing review of her book that appeared in *The Tailor & Cutter*, the real newspaper that the mouse on the cover of *The Tailor of Gloucester* is reading. One of the paper's representatives had happened to stop by a certain tailor's shop in Chelsea and was shown the book, and told of how Beatrix came in and drew the shop.

LL CUNDIFF

Norman took such an interest in Beatrix's books that for *The Tale of Two Bad Mice*, he made a house, complete with a glass observation wall for Beatrix's pet mice, Hunca-Munca and Tom Thumb (who were her models for the book's drawings). Beatrix then had the appealing thought of switching the mice's locale to the dollhouse Norman was finishing for his niece, Winifred. Together Beatrix and Norman decided how to furnish the house for the book—Norman's nieces and nephews supplied dolls, while Norman procured some "play food" for the house from an elegant store called Hamley's, along with another doll to be the cook and such important fixtures as a stove. When the dollhouse was complete, it was moved from Bedford Square to Surbiton, Fruing Warne's home. Beatrix was invited there to draw

From Ginger & Pickles, *1909*

the house, but Mrs. Potter would not have it, even when invitation was extended to both mother and daughter for lunch. Even as this oppression wore on Beatrix, she complied with her parents' demands, ever the respectful daughter. To ease the difficult situation Norman took many photographs of the dollhouse, exterior and interior, which provided Beatrix with a model for her own drawings. As with all his gestures, this was gladly received.

Both *The Tale of Two Bad Mice* and *The Tale of Benjamin Bunny* appeared in 1904; after *Benjamin*, Beatrix was somewhat tired of rabbits. She centered her next book upon her pet hedgehog, Mrs. Tiggy-Winkle, who, as she related to Norman, proved to be something of a fidget when it came to modelling: "Mrs. Tiggy as a model is comical. So long as she can go to sleep on my knee she is delighted, but if she is propped up on end for half an hour, she first begins to yawn pathetically, and then she *does* bite!"

Events came to a head in the summer of 1905. Norman's and Beatrix's friendship had deepened, and Norman proposed marriage. Beatrix accepted. This was one of the most difficult steps she had ever taken, because of the strength it took to oppose her parents. Beatrix lived in a time where the first priority was to honor, respect, and obey one's parents, no matter what their opinions. To stand against them on this matter must have felt like the greatest sin in the world, and brought Beatrix a great deal of guilt; even so, she was engaged, and her parents *knew* of her intentions, although many others did not.

Beatrix fit in at Bedford Square fairly easily, and began to feel part of the family and the warmth there. Sadly, however, late in the summer Norman was discovered to have leukemia, and died before the summer was over. Beatrix and Millie were already very close, and they helped support each other during this period, as they would continue to do in later years as well.

Beatrix in the country during her writing years

A HOME IN THE NORTH

"When we grow old and wear spectacles, our eyes are not bright, like children's eyes, nor our ears so quick, to see and hear the fairies. Just a glimpse I catch sometimes through the trees, and I hear a tinkling, tinkle, tinkling of little pots and pans and cans."

B eatrix felt it best to focus on her work, her life's remaining sustenance, and she did so, secluding herself in the northern hill country where her family had vacationed. She had bought Hill Top Farm with her own finan-ces, which had grown from her earn-ings and from an inheritance from an aunt. Beatrix had always had great af-fection for the village of Sawrey, where the farm was, and she included aspects of it in some of her books, including *The Tale of Jemima Puddle-Duck*, *The Tale of Tom Kitten*, and *Pigling Bland*.

Beatrix had been inspired in her pur-chase of the farm by Bertram, who had his own farm on the Scottish border. She wrote, "My brother and I were born in London . . . but our descent, our interest and our joy were in the north country." The times in which she lived dictated that it was improper for a woman to be unmarried and live alone, so she took to visiting the farm on occasion and leaving it in the hands of the caretaker, John Cannon, and his family, who were hard-working, honest people.

Beatrix decorated and made additions to the house when she could, and she decorated the library with her brother's paintings, all the while keeping in touch with Millie Warne. The house had many charming nooks and intricacies, as she discovered through exploration and directing workmen. Outside she maintained an interesting and varied garden of many different flowers, which she nurtured intuitively.

LL CUNDIFF

True to form, she established another animal haven, with her hedgehog, the caretaker's cats, sheep, and a family of rats she called the Whiskers. She also had chickens, and pigs, of which she made many sketches for *Pigling Bland*. Throughout all, she was learning about farming from John Cannon.

There is a saying that home is not always where you come from, and Beatrix seemed to live this out. In many ways she was cut from the same cloth as the people of Sawrey, and they accepted her. Whenever they saw her in the village, she was as unaffected as ever in her practical dress, totally unconcerned about what they may have thought of her. Life at Hill Top was comfortable and it was hers—but it became more and more trying to be limited only to visits there, still spending most of the year with her parents.

Beatrix produced thirteen books in her first eight years of just visiting Hill Top Farm, but there were other matters as well to occupy her time, such as the affairs of her already successful books. *The Tale of Peter Rabbit*, for example, was being translated into foreign languages, which Beatrix had to monitor carefully—if not done well, these translations could destroy the flavor of the books. Another large concern was copyright, as there had already been appearances in America of unauthorized versions of *Peter Rabbit*.

These occupations were of little joy to her, and Bolton Gardens became more of a prison than ever as she thought of her animals and yearned for her home in the north country. In 1909 she contacted a firm that handled property in the Sawrey area, and purchased another property, very near Hill Top, called Castle Farm. The firm of solicitors, W. Heelis & Sons, was a family-owned and -run business, well established in the area. William Heelis, the chief person she worked with on the purchase, was a native of the Lake District and understood her love for the area. He knew and was known well by all the locals, and had an excellent knowledge of the local properties. Beatrix found that his gentleness and industriousness made him a good person with whom to work; she appreciated his manner and his efforts. Together they mapped out the water supply to Castle Farm and looked after the final work, even in freezing weather.

Beatrix had to return to Bolton Gardens when she caught a

severe cold, and it took her a while to recover. William Heelis sent her many newsy and uplifting letters from the north country, and in one—to her profound ambivalence—he proposed. Beatrix was now older and less robust than she had been a decade ago, when she fought her parents for Norman, but she put herself to it, now with her brother's expressed support as well. The months of conflict that followed (for her parents, of course, objected) now affected her heart, and she became very weak. But eventually she managed to return to Hill Top to find the quiet necessary to restore her health, and at last, in the summer, she was engaged to William. They were married on October 14, 1913.

Marriage and Beatrix took to each other like long-lost old friends. She and William settled in at Castle Farm, where they were quite happy: as she wrote to Millie Warne, after less than a year of marriage, "I feel as if I had been married many years."

At this point Beatrix had stepped fully into her new life, leaving all old aspects, including the books, behind. Her old life had been so unsatisfying that she had had to create the books as a mock-fulfillment; in some ways they were just daydreams about the countryside and animals that she knew existed, but that she could not have. But she no longer needed to imagine, now that she was actually living that life.

There were just four more books that Beatrix Potter published during her married life: *Johnny Town-mouse*, in 1918 (which was more similar to the earlier books than the other three), and *The Fairy Caravan*, *Little Pig Robinson*, and *Sister Anne*, all of which appeared in 1928. There are several factors that separate this later work from the rest. A central one is her desire, after her marriage, to cut herself off from her former life and life-style, which meant separating herself from the feelings that created the earlier books. Also, her new life-style put heavy demands on her time and energy. During the first year of her marriage World War I had broken out and had taken all the manpower from the farm, so she was forced to do strenuous work on the farm and in the fields herself. While working on illustrations for *Peter Rabbit's Almanac* she wrote, " . . . these are good, but they try my eyes very much. I can't see to do them on dark days, and the lambing time is beginning, when it is not possible to neglect out-of-door affairs." She wrote later, "I am written out for story books, and my eyes are tired for painting." More than anything, it seemed that Beatrix's best period of creativity was over, and she knew it was time to devote herself to a new life.

From The Pie and the Patty Pan, *1905*

THE MOST IMPORTANT GIFT

"There is a strong desire among thoughtful people to preserve what is possible before it is too late."

It is fitting that in her later life Beatrix gave much back to the Lake District, in which she experienced her happiest moments in childhood. Because of its natural beauty, the Lake District was in danger of being over-developed by builders who hoped to make it into a prosperous vacation area. Beatrix fought the threat of development by donating money to the National Trust, a publicly funded organization that purchases land specifically to preserve its beauty. After initially buying real estate for her own satisfaction, Beatrix began buying with the Trust in mind, and in the course of her life

From The Tale of Little Pig Robinson, *1930*

secured a great number of properties in the Lake District, many of special beauty, to which her husband had helped her gain access. In total she willed about 4,000 acres to the National Trust; she acted as caretaker for many of these gifts until, after a bout with bronchitis, she passed away on December 22, 1943. Her home at Hill Top Farm was given to the National Trust after her death, and stays open during summers to visitors who want to see how she lived.

While Beatrix Potter did not produce any more children's books in the last fifteen years of her life, she ended up devoting herself to the nature she had always loved. From being a shy, unassuming young woman who wrote and drew pictures in solitude, she went on to become a well-respected member of the community whose efforts to save the land around her served countless others.

But, without a doubt, Beatrix Potter will be remembered for her delicate and captivating picture books. We will always admire her for the secret, individual world she created out of loneliness. Her ability to capture both the realistic and the magical in the animal world seems to speak directly to all our imaginations, and assures us that Beatrix Potter's work will continue to charm readers for generations to come.

A Selected Reading List

Books by Beatrix Potter

The Tale of Peter Rabbit
The Tale of Benjamin Bunny
The Tale of Mrs. Tiggy-Winkle
The Tale of Tom Kitten
The Tale of Squirrel Nutkin
The Tale of Mr. Jeremy Fisher
The Tale of Two Bad Mice
The Roly-Poly Pudding
Cecily Parsley's Nursery Rhymes
Letters to Children

Books about Beatrix Potter

Beatrix Potter: Children's Storyteller, by Patricia Dendtler Frevert, Creative Editions, 1981
The Magic Years of Beatrix Potter, by Margaret Lane, Warne, 1978
The Art of Beatrix Potter, by Beatrix Potter, Warne, 1972
A History of the Writings of Beatrix Potter, by L. Linder, Warne, 1971
Nothing Is Impossible: The Story of Beatrix Potter, by Dorothy Aldis, Atheneum, 1969
The Tale of Beatrix Potter: A Biography, by Marcia Dalphin, Warne, 1948